Painting and Quote from his Book
Our Future?
Rowland C. Marshall

The Spark of the Divine

German Philosopher Hegel,
Remarked that the
Spark of the Divine
is within the individual person.
If that is true, it would follow that
every child, youth, or adult
human is of infinite value.

Foreword

Hymns, including Greek and Latin, the psalter or book of psalms, ancient chant, early canticles, spirituals, and contemporary gospel, have created a hymnody, which over many centuries has become the most profound vehicle for praise and worship in the Christian Church. It has once been said that the Church, "Has come singing down through the ages". Through this beautiful medium of song, worshippers over many generations have privately and collectively aspired to give praise and proclaim their faith while expressing the higher emotions of the soul.

My dear son, Christian Davidson, who was himself a composer and arranger, was the inspiration behind this book. Christian had a particular fondness for the works of Johann Sebastian Bach. In particular, Bach's Cantata number 140, which was based on the hymn Sleepers Awake written in 1598 by Philipp Nicolai. Sleepers Awake became the title of this book of twenty hymn arrangements for the classical guitarist after ten years since the commencement of this project.

After several months during 2006 twenty arrangements were completed. However, the project stalled and was not to be revived for a decade when, almost to the day, a new student came through my studio door wishing to study classical guitar. Her encouragement and grace motivated me to revisit the project and bring it to fruition. I have dedicated this book to Terry-Lynn Mireault for her timely spiritual support and interest as well her contribution to the proofreading of Sleepers Awake.

The first twenty arrangements were carefully written with much consideration given to the original four-part choral arrangements found in several of the more popular hymn books available. Some of these arrangements were personalized based on my own tastes and compositional ideas. As these arrangements would challenge many of the seasoned players I felt it would be appropriate to provide twenty more arrangements of the same hymns as an option. I then went further by adding another twenty arrangements, again of the same hymns, as accompaniment to a vocal line with lyrics. With sixty original arrangements, it is my desire to allow as many as possible to enjoy the beauty and peace of these wonderful melodies.

I wish to thank, Ben Robertson, for his assistance as editorial advisor. I also wish to express my gratitude to Rowland Marshall for the use of his artwork and quotes throughout the book.

Kenneth Michael Davidson
October 2016

Copyright 2016 © Kenneth Michael Davidson

All Rights Reserved. No part of this book may be reproduced or transmitted in any form by any means without permission in writing by the publisher.

Published in Canada by Kenneth Michael Davidson
Nova Scotia, Canada
macdhaimusic@gmail.com

Library and Archives Canada Cataloguing in Publication

ISBN-13: 9780995810709
ISBN-10: 0995810702

Acknowledgments

Christian Davidson – His Inspiration and Title of this Book

Ben Robertson – Music Editorial Advisor

Rowland C. Marshall – Original Artwork and Quotes

Terry-Lynn Mireault – Proofreader and Spiritual Consultant

Cover Photo – Hanika 60 Classical

10 9 8 7 6 5 4 3 2 1   21 20 19 18 17

Dedicated to:

Terry-Lynn Mireault
For her Spiritual Support and Guidance

Index of Hymns

1	Abide With Me	6
2	Holy, Holy, Holy	10
3	Immortal, Invisible, God Only Wise	14
4	In The Garden	18
5	Shall We Gather At The River	22
6	The Lord Is My Shepherd	26
7	Thine Be The Glory	30
8	The Old Rugged Cross	34
9	Infant Holy, Infant Lowly	40
10	Rejoice, The Lord Is King	44
11	We Gather Together	48
12	Blessed Assurance	52
13	All For Jesus	56
14	He Leadeth Me O Blessed Thought	60
15	Jesus, Thou Joy Of Loving Hearts	64
16	Amazing Grace	68
17	Alleluia! Sing To Jesus	72
18	This Is My Father's World	76
19	Easter Hymn	80
20	Chorale from Cantata No. 140 (Sleepers Awake)	84

Dancing the tune
Toasting the moon
Sing us another one,
Sing us another one – do

Excerpt from, Sing Us A Song
Rowland C. Marshall

1a Abide With Me

Henry F. Lyte - William F. Monk

Arrangement Copyright © Kenneth Michael Davidson 2016

1b Abide With Me

Henry F. Lyte - William H. Monk

Arrangement Copyright © Kenneth Michael Davidson 2016

1c Abide With Me

Henry F. Lyte - William H. Monk

Arrangement Copyright © Kenneth Michael Davidson 2016

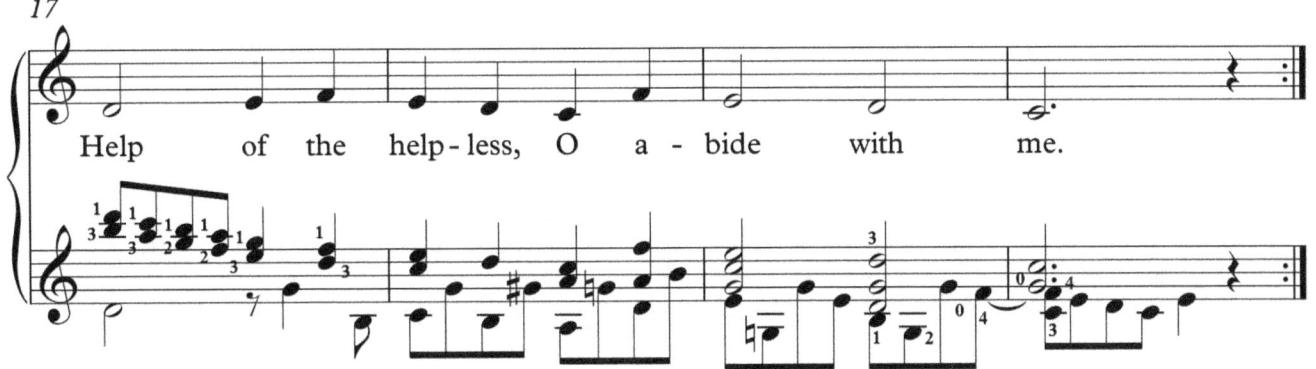

Help of the help-less, O a-bide with me.

Swift to its close ebbs out life's little day;
Earth's joys grow dim; its glories pass away;
Change and decay in all around I see;
O Thou who changest not, abide with me.

Not a brief glance I beg, a passing word;
But as Thou dwell'st with Thy disciples, Lord,
Familiar, condescending, patient, free.
Come not to sojourn, but abide with me.

Come not in terrors, as the King of kings,
But kind and good, with healing in Thy wings,
Tears for all woes, a heart for every plea—
Come, Friend of sinners, and thus bide with me.

Thou on my head in early youth didst smile;
And, though rebellious and perverse meanwhile,
Thou hast not left me, oft as I left Thee,
On to the close, O Lord, abide with me.

I need Thy presence every passing hour.
What but Thy grace can foil the tempter's power?
Who, like Thyself, my guide and stay can be?
Through cloud and sunshine, Lord, abide with me.

I fear no foe, with Thee at hand to bless;
Ills have no weight, and tears no bitterness.
Where is death's sting? Where, grave, thy victory?
I triumph still, if Thou abide with me.

Hold Thou Thy cross before my closing eyes;
Shine through the gloom and point me to the skies.
Heaven's morning breaks, and earth's vain shadows flee;
In life, in death, O Lord, abide with me.

2a Holy, Holy, Holy

Reginald Heber - John B. Dykes
1783 - 1826   1861

Arrangement Copyright © Kenneth Michael Davidson 2016

2b Holy, Holy, Holy

Reginald Heber - John B. Dykes
1783 - 1826   1861

Arrangement Copyright © Kenneth Michael Davidson 2016

Holy, holy, holy! All the saints adore Thee,
Casting down their golden crowns around the glassy sea;
Cherubim and seraphim falling down before Thee,
Who was, and is, and evermore shall be.

Holy, holy, holy! Though the darkness hide Thee,
Though the eye of sinful man Thy glory may not see;
Only Thou art holy; there is none beside Thee,
Perfect in power, in love, and purity.

Holy, holy, holy! Lord God Almighty!
All Thy works shall praise Thy Name, in earth, and sky, and sea;
Holy, holy, holy; merciful and mighty!
God in three Persons, blessed Trinity!

3a Immortal, Invisible, God Only Wise
Walter C. Smith 1867

3b Immortal, Invisible, God Only Wise
Walter C. Smith 1867

Arrangement Copyright © Kenneth Michael Davidson 2016

3c Immortal, Invisible, God Only Wise
Walter C. Smith 1867 m

Arrangement Copyright © Kenneth Michael Davidson 2016

Unresting, unhasting, and silent as light,
Nor wanting, nor wasting, thou rulest in might;
Thy justice like mountains high soaring above
Thy clouds which are fountains of goodness and love.

To all life thou givest to both great and small;
In all life thou livest, the true life of all;
We blossom and flourish as leaves on the tree,
And wither and perish but nought changeth thee.

Great Father of glory, pure Father of light,
Thine angels adore thee, all veiling their sight;

4a In The Garden
C. Austin Miles

4b In The Garden
C. Austin Miles

4c In The Garden
C. Audtin Miles

He speaks, and the sound of His voice
Is so sweet the birds hush their singing,
And the melody that He gave to me
Within my heart is ringing.

Refrain

I'd stay in the garden with Him
Though the night around me be falling,
But He bids me go: through the voice of woe
His voice to me is calling.

Refrain

5a Shall We Gather At The River
Robert Lowry

5b Shall We Gather At The River
Robert Lowry

Arrangement Copyright © Kenneth Michael Davidson 2016

5c Shall We Gather At The River
Robert Lowry

On the margin of the river,
Washing up its silver spray,
We will talk and worship ever,
All the happy golden day. *Refrain*

Ere we reach the shining river,
Lay we every burden down;
Grace our spirits will deliver,
And provide a robe and crown. *Refrain*

At the smiling of the river,
Mirror of the Savior's face,
Saints, whom death will never sever,
Lift their songs of saving grace. *Refrain*

Soon we'll reach the silver river,
Soon our pilgrimage will cease;
Soon our happy hearts will quiver
With the melody of peace. *Refrain*

6a The Lord Is My Shepherd

From Psalm 23 - Jessie Seymour Irvine

Arrangement Copyright © Kenneth Michael Davidson 2016

6b The Lord Is My Shepherd

From Psalm 23 - Jesse Seymour Irvine

Arrangement Copyright © Kenneth Michael Davidson 2016

6c The Lord Is My Shepherd

From Psalm 23 - Jesse Seymore Irvine

Arrangement Copyright © Kenneth Michael Davidson 2016

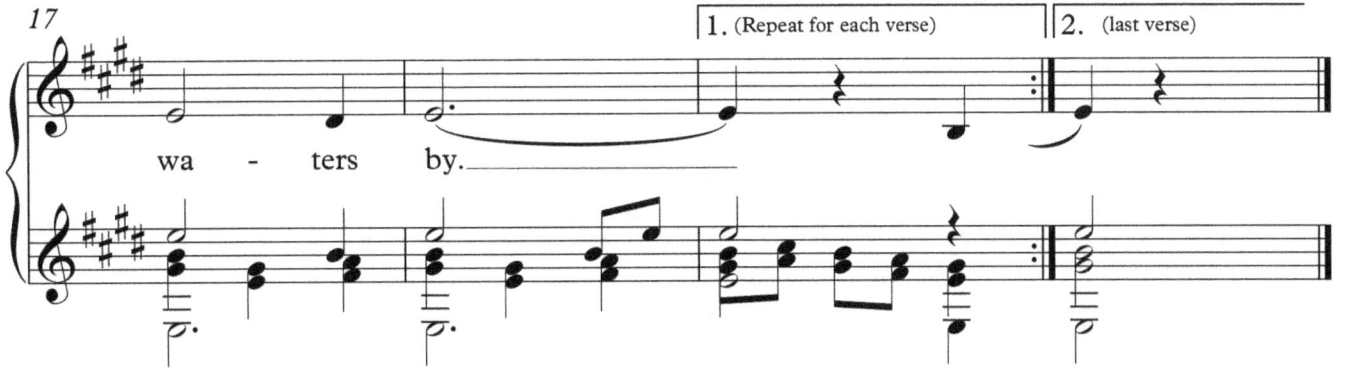

My soul he doth restore again,
And me to walk doth make
Within the paths of righteousness,
E'en for his own name's sake.

Yea, though I walk in death's dark vale,
Yet will I fear no ill:
For thou art with me, and thy rod
And staff me comfort still.

My table thou hast furnished
In presence of my foes;
My head thou dost with oil anoint
And my cup overflows.

Goodness and mercy all my life
Shall surely follow me;
And in God's house for evermore
My dwelling-place shall be.

7a   Thine Be The Glory
George Frederick Handel

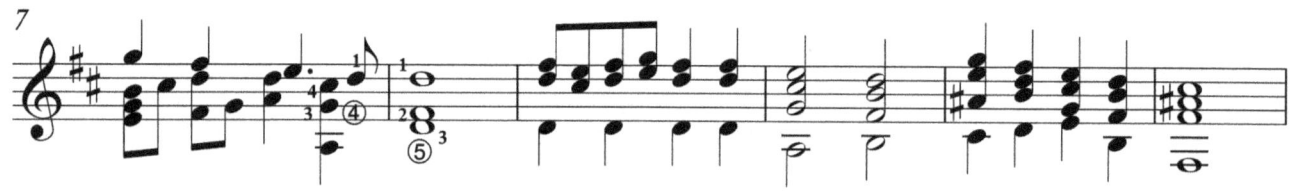

7b Thine Be The Glory

George Frederick Handel

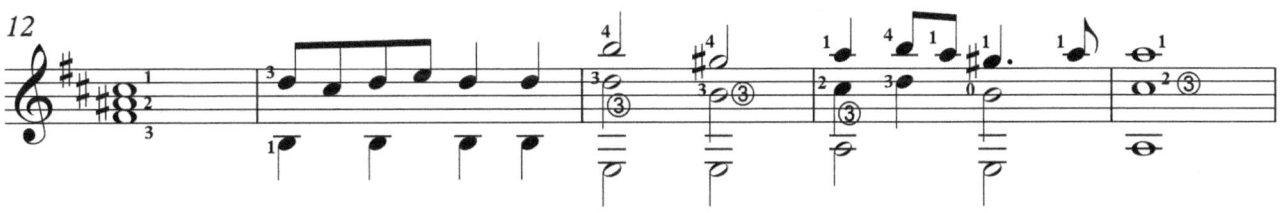

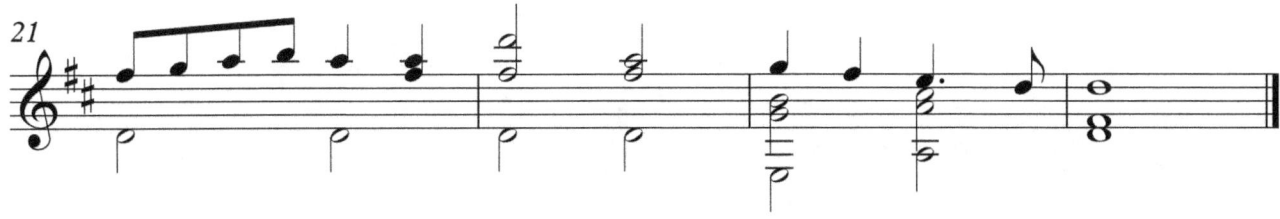

Arrangement Copyright © Kenneth Michael Davidson 2016

7c Thine Be The Glory

George Frederick Handel

Arrangement Copyright © Kenneth Michael Davidson 2016

Lo! Jesus meets us, risen from the tomb;
Lovingly He greets us, scatters fear and gloom;
Let the church with gladness, hymns of triumph sing;
For her Lord now liveth, death hast lost its sting.

Refrain

No more we doubt Thee, glorious Prince of life;
Life is naught without Thee; aid us in our strife;
Make us more than conquerors, through Thy deathless love;
Bring us safe through Jordan to thy home above.

Refrain

8a The Old Rugged Cross
George Bennard

8b The Old Rugged Cross
George Bennard

8c The Old Rugged Cross
George Bennard

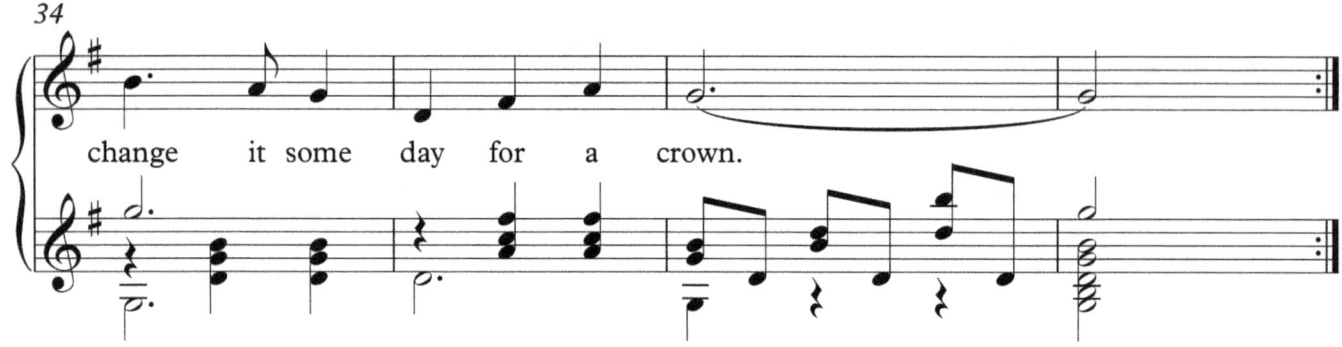

O that old rugged cross, so despised by the world,
Has a wondrous attraction for me;
For the dear Lamb of God left His glory above
To bear it to dark Calvary.

Refrain

In that old rugged cross, stained with blood so divine,
A wondrous beauty I see,
For 'twas on that old cross Jesus suffered and died,
To pardon and sanctify me.

Refrain

To the old rugged cross I will ever be true;
Its shame and reproach gladly bear;
Then He'll call me some day to my home far away,
Where His glory forever I'll share.

Refrain

Ephesians 5:18–19
…be filled with the Spirit, addressing one another in psalms and hymns and spiritual songs, singing and making melody to the Lord with your heart,

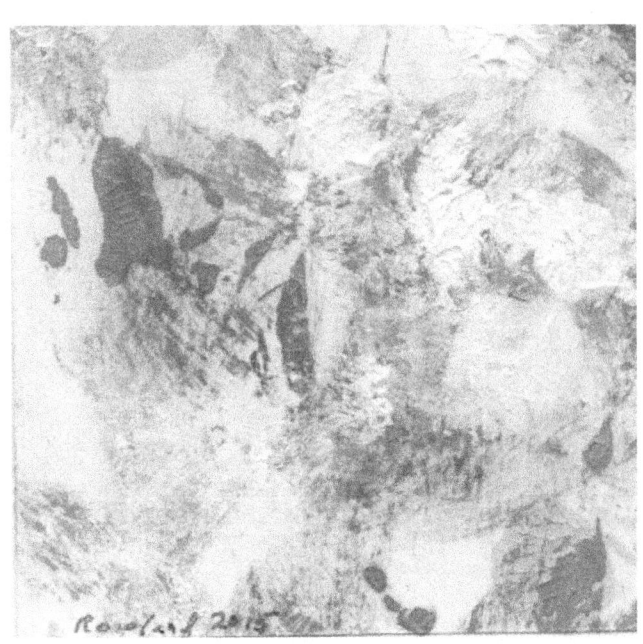

9a Infant Holy, Infant Lowly

Polish Carol - W. Zlobie Lezy - E. M. G. Reed 1933

9b Infant Holy, Infant Lowly
Polish Carol - W. Zlobie Lezy - E. M. G. Reed 1933

9c Infant Holy, Infant Lowly

Polish Carol - W. Zlobie Lezy - E. M. G. Reed 1933

Moderato

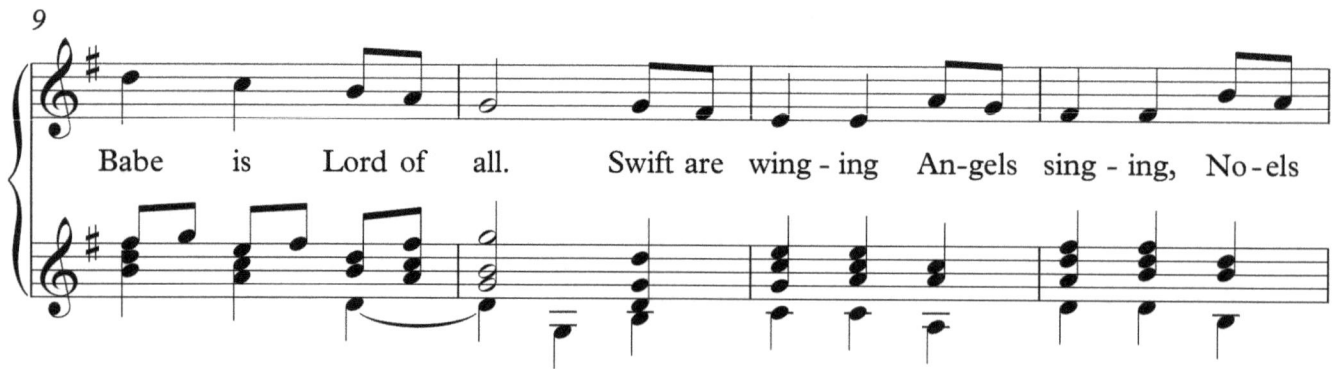

Arrangement Copyright © Kenneth Michael Davidson 2016

Flocks were sleeping, shepherds keeping
Vigil till the morning new
Saw the glory, heard the story,
Tidings of a Gospel true.

Thus rejoicing, free from sorrow,
Praises voicing, greet the morrow:
Christ the Babe was born for you.
Christ the Babe was born for you.

10a Rejoice, The Lord Is King
Charles Wesley 1746 - John Darwall 1779

Arrangement Copyright © Kenneth Michael Davidson 2016

10b Rejoice, The Lord Is King
Charles Wesley 1746 - John Darwall 1779

Arrangement Copyright © Kenneth Michael Davidson 2016

10c Rejoice, The Lord Is King
Charles Wesley 1746 - John Darwall 1779

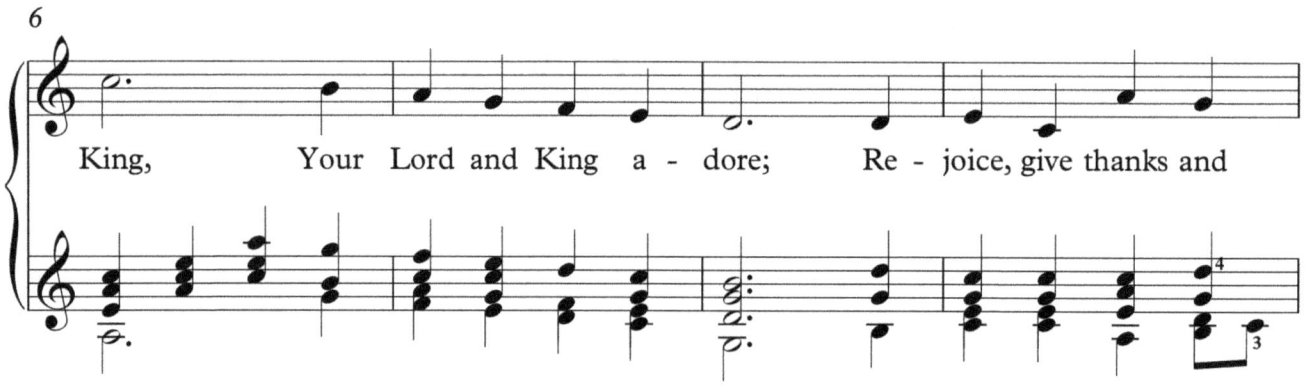

Arrangement Copyright © Kenneth Michael Davidson 2016

Jesus, the Saviour, reigns,
The God of truth and love.
When He had purged our stains,
He took His seat above.

Refrain

His Kingdom cannot fail,
He rules o'er earth and heaven.
The keys of death and hell,
Are to our Jesus given.

Refrain

He sits at God's right hand,
Till all His foes submit;
And bow to His command,
And fall beneath His feet.

Refrain

Rejoice in glorious hope!
Our Lord, the judge shall come,
And take His servant up,
To their eternal home.

Refrain

11a We Gather Together

Netherlands Folk Song

Arrangement Copyright © Kenneth Michael Davidson

11b We Gather Together
Netherlands Folk Song

Arrangement Copyright © Kenneth Michael Davidson

11c We Gather Together

Netherlands Folk Song

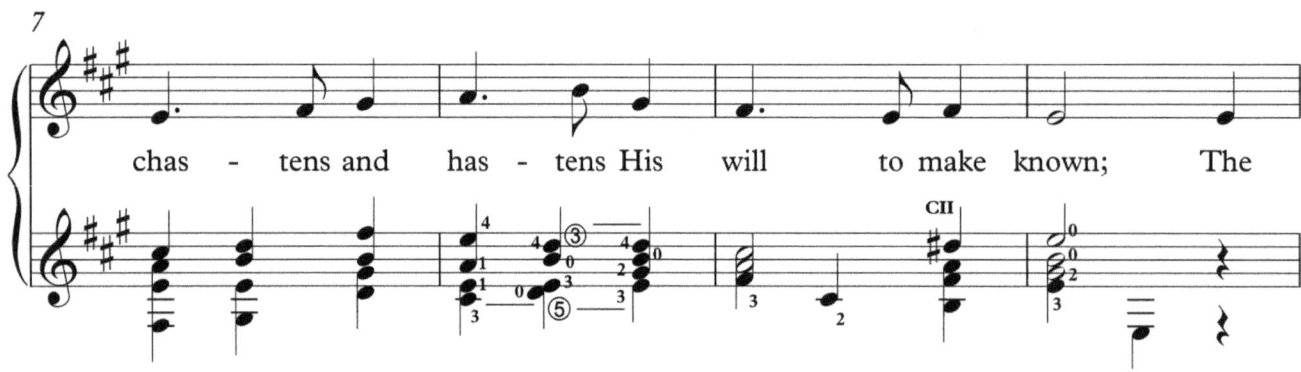

Arrangement Copyright © Kenneth Michael Davidson

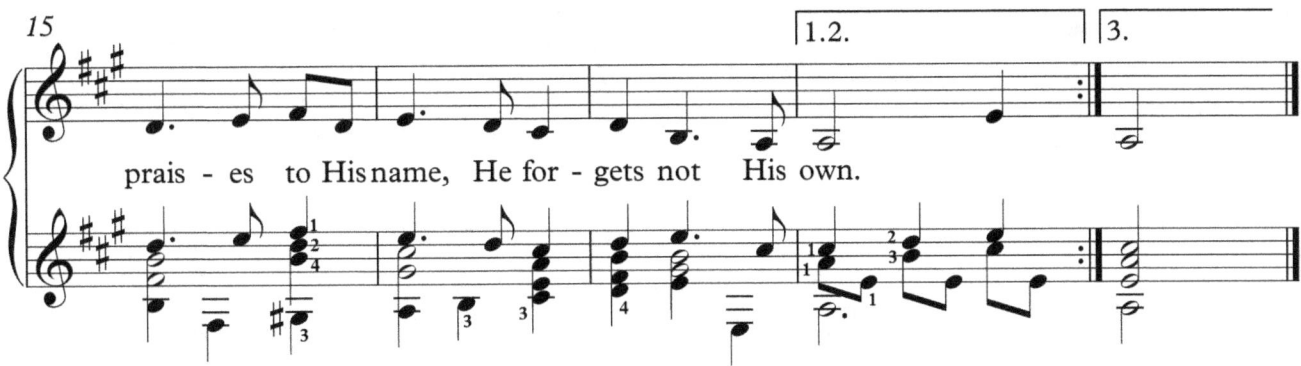

Beside us to guide us, our God with us joining,
Ordaining, maintaining His kingdom divine;
So from the beginning the fight we were winning;
Thou, Lord, were at our side, all glory be Thine!

We all do extol Thee, Thou Leader triumphant,
And pray that Thou still our Defender will be.
Let Thy congregation escape tribulation;
Thy Name be ever praised! O Lord, make us free!

12a Blessed Assurance

Fanny J. Crosby - Phoebe P. Knapp

Arrangement Copyright © Kenneth Michael Davidson 2016

12b Blessed Assurance

Fanny J. Crosby - Phoebe P. Knapp

Arrangement Copyright © Kenneth Michael Davidson 2016

12c Blessed Assurance

Fanny J. Crosby - Phoebe P. Knapp

Arrangement Copyright © Kenneth Michael Davidson 2016

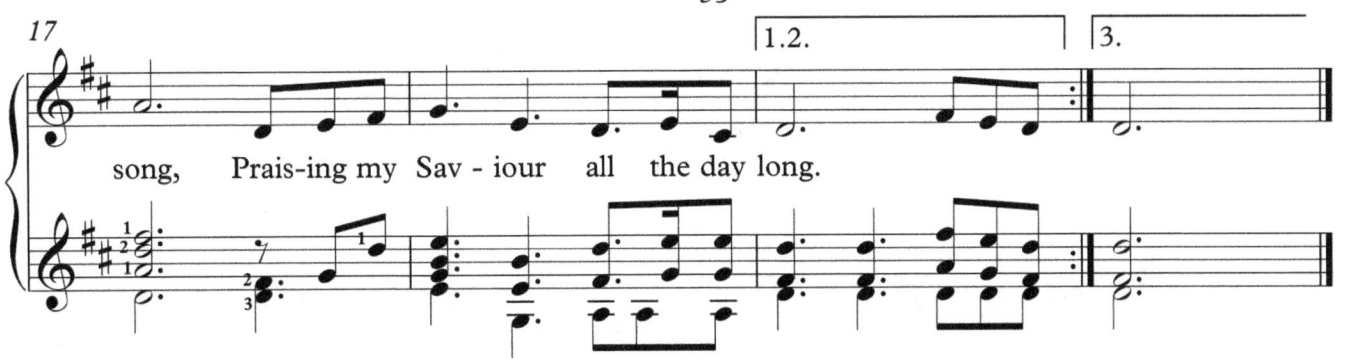

Perfect submission, perfect delight,
Visions of rapture now burst on my sight;
Angels descending bring from above
Echoes of mercy, whispers of love.

Refrain

Perfect submission, all is at rest,
I in my Saviour am happy and blest,
Watching and waiting, looking above,
Filled with His goodness, lost in His love.

Refrain

13a All For Jesus

Mary D. James - Asa Hull

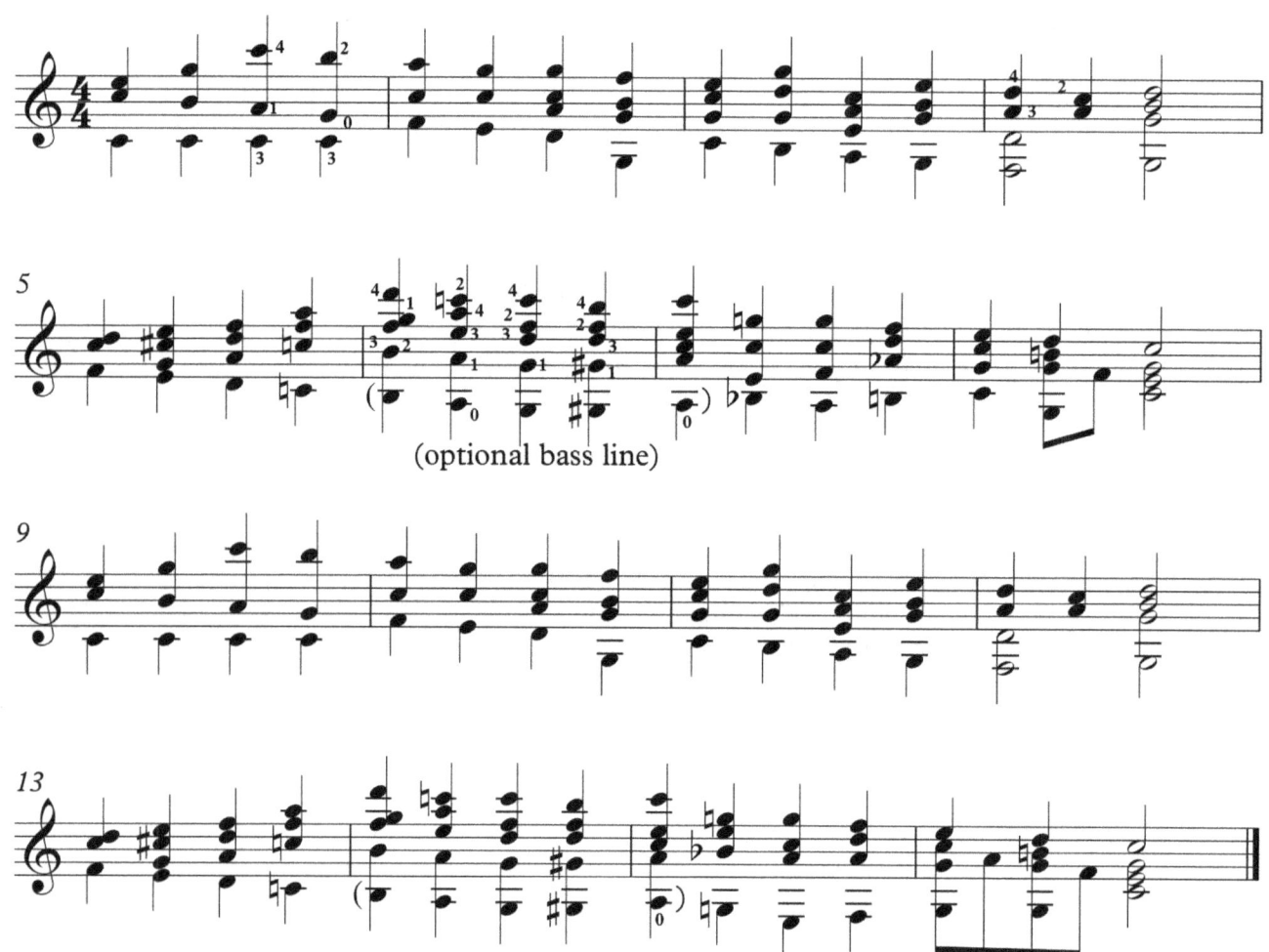

(optional bass line)

13b All For Jesus

Mary D. James - Asa Hull

Arrangement Copyright © Kenneth Michael Davidson 2016

13c All For Jesus

Mary D. James - Asa Hull

Arrangement Copyright © Kenneth Michael Davidson 2016

Let my hands perform His bidding,
Let my feet run in His ways;
Let my eyes see Jesus only,
Let my lips speak forth His praise.

Refrain

Worldlings prize their gems of beauty,
Cling to gilded toys of dust,
Boast of wealth and fame and pleasure;
Only Jesus will I trust.

Refrain

Since my eyes were fixed on Jesus,
I've lost sight of all beside;
So enchained my spirit's vision,
Looking at the Crucified.

Refrain

Oh, what wonder! how amazing!
Jesus, glorious King of kings,
Deigns to call me His belovèd,
Lets me rest beneath His wings.

Refrain

14a He Leadeth Me: O Blessed Thought

Joseph H. Gilmore 1862 - William B. Bradbury 1864

Arrangement Copyright © Kenneth Michael Davidson 2016

14b He Leadeth Me: O Blessed Thought

Joseph H. Gilmore 1862 - William B. Bradbury 1864

Arrangement Copyright © Kenneth Michael Davidson 2016

14c He Leadeth Me: O Blessed Thought

Joseph H. Gilmore 1862 - William B. Bradbury 1864

Arrangement Copyright © Kenneth Michael Davidson 2016

Sometimes 'mid scenes of deepest gloom,
Sometimes where Eden's bowers bloom,
By waters still, o'er troubled sea,
Still 'tis His hand that leadeth me.Lord,

Refrain

Lord, I would place my hand in Thine,
Nor ever murmur nor repine;
Content, whatever lot I see,
Since 'tis my God that leadeth me.

Refrain

And when my task on earth is done,
When by Thy grace the victory's won,
Even death's cold wave I will not flee,
Since God through Jordan leadeth me.

Refrain

15a Jesus, Thou Joy Of Loving Hearts

Music: Henry Baker - 1854 - Words: Bernard of Clairvaux, 12th Century

15b Jesus, Thou Joy Of Loving Hearts

Music: Henry Baker - 1854 - Words: Bernard of Clairvaux, 12th Century

15c Jesus, Thou Joy Of Loving Hearts

Music: Henry Baker - 1854 - Words: Bernard of Clairvaux, 12th Century

we turn un-filled to Thee a-gain.

Thy truth unchanged hath ever stood;
Thou savest those that on Thee call;
To them that seek Thee Thou art good,
To them that find Thee all in all.

We taste Thee, O Thou living Bread,
And long to feast upon Thee still;
We drink of Thee, the Fountainhead,
And thirst our souls from Thee to fill.

Our restless spirits yearn for Thee,
Wherever our changeful lot is cast;
Glad when Thy gracious smile we see,
Blessed when our faith can hold Thee fast.

O Jesus, ever with us stay,
Make all our moments calm and bright;
Chase the dark night of sin away,
Shed over the world Thy holy light.

16a Amazing Grace
John Newton

Arrangement Copyright © Kenneth Michael Davidson 2016

16b Amazing Grace
John Newton

Arrangement Copyright © Kenneth Michael Davidson 2016

16c Amazing Grace
John Newton

Arrangement Copyright © Kenneth Michael Davidson 2016

'Twas grace that taught my heart to fear,
And grace my fears relieved;
How precious did that grace appear
The hour I first believed.

Through many dangers, toils and snares,
I have already come;
'Tis grace hath brought me safe thus far,
And grace will lead me home.

The Lord has promised good to me,
His word my hope secures;
He will my shield and portion be,
As long as life endures.

Yea, when this flesh and heart shall fail,
And mortal life shall cease,
I shall possess, within the veil,
A life of joy and peace.

The world shall soon dissolve like snow,
The sun refuse to shine;
But God, who called me here below,
Shall be forever mine.

When we've been there ten thousand years,
Bright shining as the sun,
We've no less days to sing God's praise
Than when we'd first begun.

17a Alleluia! Sing To Jesus

William C. Dix 1866 - Rowland H. Prichard 1830

17b Alleluia! Sing To Jesus

William C. Dix 1866 - Rowland H. Prichard 1830

Arrangement Copyright © Kenneth Michael Davidson 2016

17c Alleluia! Sing To Jesus
William C. Dix 1866 - Rowland H. Prichard 1830

Arrangement Copyright © Kenneth Michael Davidson 2016

Alleluia! Not as orphans, Are we left in sorrow now;
Alleluia! He is near us; Faith believes, nor questions how.
Though the cloud from sight received Him, When the forty days were o'er,
Shall our hearts forget His promise? — "I am with you evermore."

Alleluia! Bread of angels, Here on earth our Food, our Stay;
Alleluia! Here the humble, Flee to You from day to day.
Advocate and Intercessor, Earth's Redeemer, hear our plea;
You, the Lamb, alone we worship, You, the Lamb, alone we see.

Alleluia! King eternal, Lord omnipotent we own;
Alleluia! Born of Mary, Earth Your footstool, Heav'n Your throne.
Robed in flesh, the veil You sundered, Limitless High Priest we laud—
You have saved us from destruction, You have raised us up to God!

18a This Is My Father's World
Traditional English Melody

Arrangement Copyright © Kenneth Michael Davidson 2016

18b This Is My Father's World
Traditional English Melody

18c   This Is My Father's World

Traditional English Melody

Arrangement Copyright © Kenneth Michael Davidson 2016

This is my Father's world,
the birds their carols raise,
the morning light, the lily white,
declare their maker's praise.
This is my Father's world:
he shines in all that's fair;
in the rustling grass I hear him pass;
he speaks to me everywhere.

This is my Father's world.
O let me ne'er forget
that though the wrong seems oft so strong,
God is the ruler yet.
This is my Father's world:
why should my heart be sad?
The Lord is King; let the heavens ring!
God reigns; let the earth be glad!

19a   Easter Hymn

Charles Wesley 1739 - Lyra Davidica 1708

19b Easter Hymn

Charles Wesley 1739 - Lyra Davidica 1708

19c Easter Hymn
Charles Wesley 1739 - Lyra Davidica 1708

Arrangement Copyright © Kenneth Michael Davidson 2016

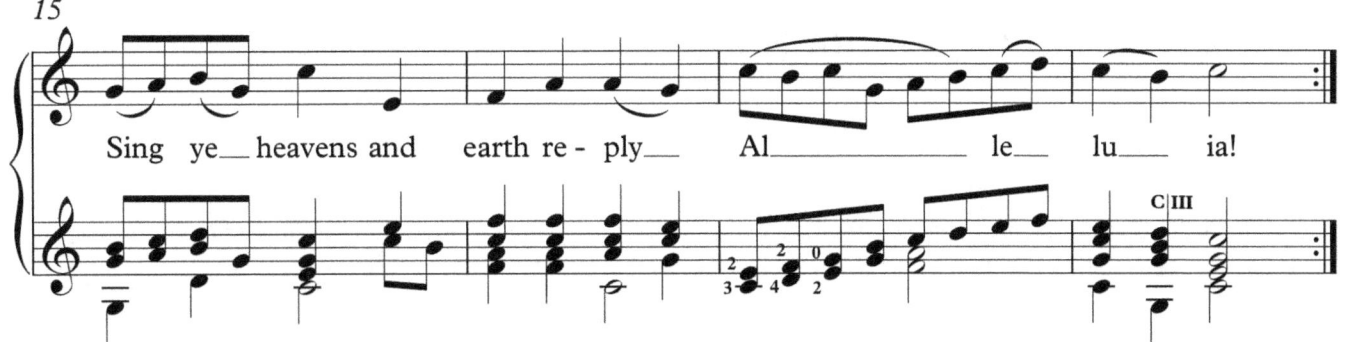

Love's redeeming work is done, Alleluia!
Fought the fight, the battle won, Alleluia!
Death in vain forbids him rise, Alleluia!
Christ has opened paradise, Alleluia!

Lives again our glorious King, Alleluia!
Where, O death, is now thy sting? Alleluia!
Once he died our souls to save, Alleluia!
Where's thy victory, boasting grave? Alleluia!

Soar we now where Christ has led, Alleluia!
Following our exalted Head, Alleluia!
Made like him, like him we rise, Alleluia!
Ours the cross, the grave, the skies, Alleluia!

Hail the Lord of earth and heaven, Alleluia!
Praise to thee by both be given, Alleluia!
Thee we greet triumphant now, Alleluia!
Hail the Resurrection, thou, Alleluia!

King of glory, soul of bliss, Alleluia!
Everlasting life is this, Alleluia!
Thee to know, thy power to prove, Alleluia!
Thus to sing, and thus to love, Alleluia!

20a Wachet auf, uns die Stimme

(Sleepers Awake) Philipp Nicolai 1598
Chorale from Cantata No. 140 - Johann Sebastian Bach

20b Wachet auf, uns die Stimme

(Sleepers Awake) Philipp Nicolai 1598
Chorale from Cantata No. 140 - Johann Sebastian Bach

Arrangement Copyright © Kenneth Michael Davidson 2016

20c Wachet auf, uns die Stimme

(Sleepers Awake) Philipp Nicolai 1598
Chorale from Cantata No. 140 - Johann Sebastian Bach

Arrangement Copyright © Kenneth Michael Davidson 2016

Late 19th Century Church Choir

 Kenneth Michael Davidson first began playing publically as a classical guitarist in the mid 1960s at Canadian Martyrs Parish Church in Ottawa. Following classical guitar studies with Stephan Fentock of McGill University Kenneth continued studies at Dalhousie University in Halifax 1973 – 1977 under renowned classical guitar professor, Carl (Carol) van Feggelen. For more than a decade Kenneth performed with a small chamber group and choir at Saint John Vianney Church in Lower Sackville, Nova Scotia.

Currently a regular speaker and clinician for the Nova Scotia Music Educators Association, guitar curriculum writer for the Nova Scotia Department of Education with a provincially approved guitar text book used in public schools, writer of Guitar Explorations and Become The Guitar for the Nova Scotia Community College, and decades of music teaching in the public school systems in three provinces, two universities and two conservatories. And with almost three decades teaching classical guitar and guitar in music therapy at Acadia University, Kenneth's pedagogical methods have been widely accepted and refined to culminate in a desire to assist guitarists not only in their role as performer but also as caregivers, music therapists, educators, and as people helping people wherever they may find an opportunity to share their gift of music.

www.ingramcontent.com/pod-product-compliance
Lightning Source LLC
Chambersburg PA
CBHW081219230426
43666CB00015B/2798